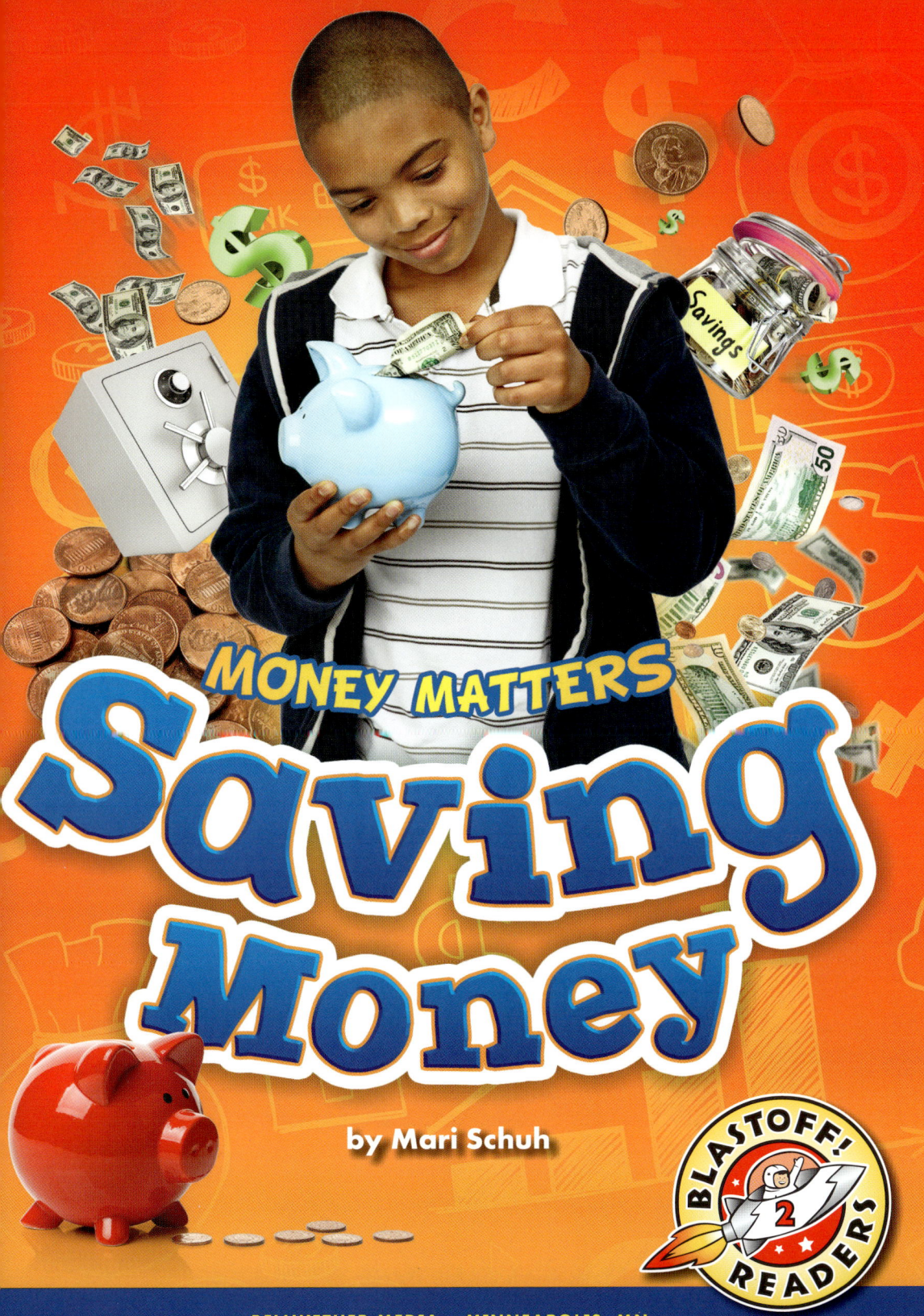

Note to Librarians, Teachers, and Parents:

Blastoff! Readers are carefully developed by literacy experts and combine standards-based content with developmentally appropriate text.

Level 1 provides the most support through repetition of high-frequency words, light text, predictable sentence patterns, and strong visual support.

Level 2 offers early readers a bit more challenge through varied simple sentences, increased text load, and less repetition of high-frequency words.

Level 3 advances early-fluent readers toward fluency through increased text and concept load, less reliance on visuals, longer sentences, and more literary language.

Level 4 builds reading stamina by providing more text per page, increased use of punctuation, greater variation in sentence patterns, and increasingly challenging vocabulary.

Level 5 encourages children to move from "learning to read" to "reading to learn" by providing even more text, varied writing styles, and less familiar topics.

Whichever book is right for your reader, Blastoff! Readers are the perfect books to build confidence and encourage a love of reading that will last a lifetime!

This edition first published in 2016 by Bellwether Media, Inc.

No part of this publication may be reproduced in whole or in part without written permission of the publisher. For information regarding permission, write to Bellwether Media, Inc., Attention: Permissions Department, 5357 Penn Avenue South, Minneapolis, MN 55419.

Library of Congress Cataloging-in-Publication Data

Schuh, Mari C., 1975-
  Saving Money / by Mari Schuh.
    pages cm. – (Blastoff! Readers: Money Matters)
  Summary: "Relevant images match informative text in this introduction to saving money. Intended for students in kindergarten through third grade"– Provided by publisher.
  Audience: Ages 5-8
  Audience: K to grade 3
  Includes bibliographical references and index.
  ISBN 978-1-62617-247-0 (hardcover: alk. paper)
  1. Saving and investment–Juvenile literature. 2. Children–Finance, Personal–Juvenile literature. I. Title.
  HB822.S38 2016
  332.024–dc23
                2015004751

Text copyright © 2016 by Bellwether Media, Inc. BLASTOFF! READERS and associated logos are trademarks and/or registered trademarks of Bellwether Media, Inc. SCHOLASTIC, CHILDREN'S PRESS, and associated logos are trademarks and/or registered trademarks of Scholastic Inc.

Printed in the United States of America, North Mankato, MN.

Table of Contents

Why Save Money?	4
Ways to Save Money	10
Saving Is Smart	20
Glossary	22
To Learn More	23
Index	24

Why Save Money?

Why do people save money? People save money so they can use it in the future.

Then they can buy things they **need** and **want**. They are also prepared for unplanned costs.

Some people save money until they reach a **goal**. They save enough money to buy what they want.

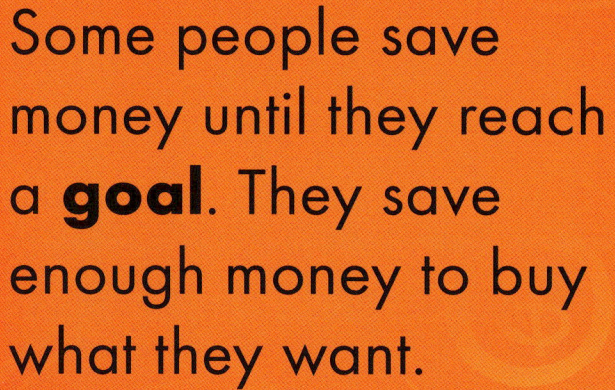

Some people save money for **sales**. Then they spend less money on what they buy.

Adults often save money in an **emergency fund**.

They use the money for doctor visits, car repairs, and house projects.

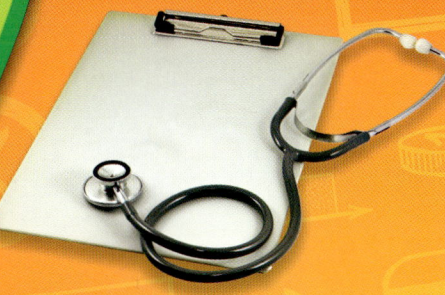
doctor visits

car repairs

house projects

Ways to Save Money

Kids can save money, too.

They can put money they earn and receive in a piggy bank.

Some kids save all the money they earn. Other kids spend some money and save the rest.

Some people put money into a **savings account** at their **bank**.

They can take money out of the account at any time.

Some people buy **savings bonds** from the United States government.

Savings bonds earn money for a certain length of time.

Savings accounts and savings bonds grow over time.

The money grows because it earns **interest**.

Saving Is Smart

It is smart to save money. People who save can pay for a house, college, and trips.

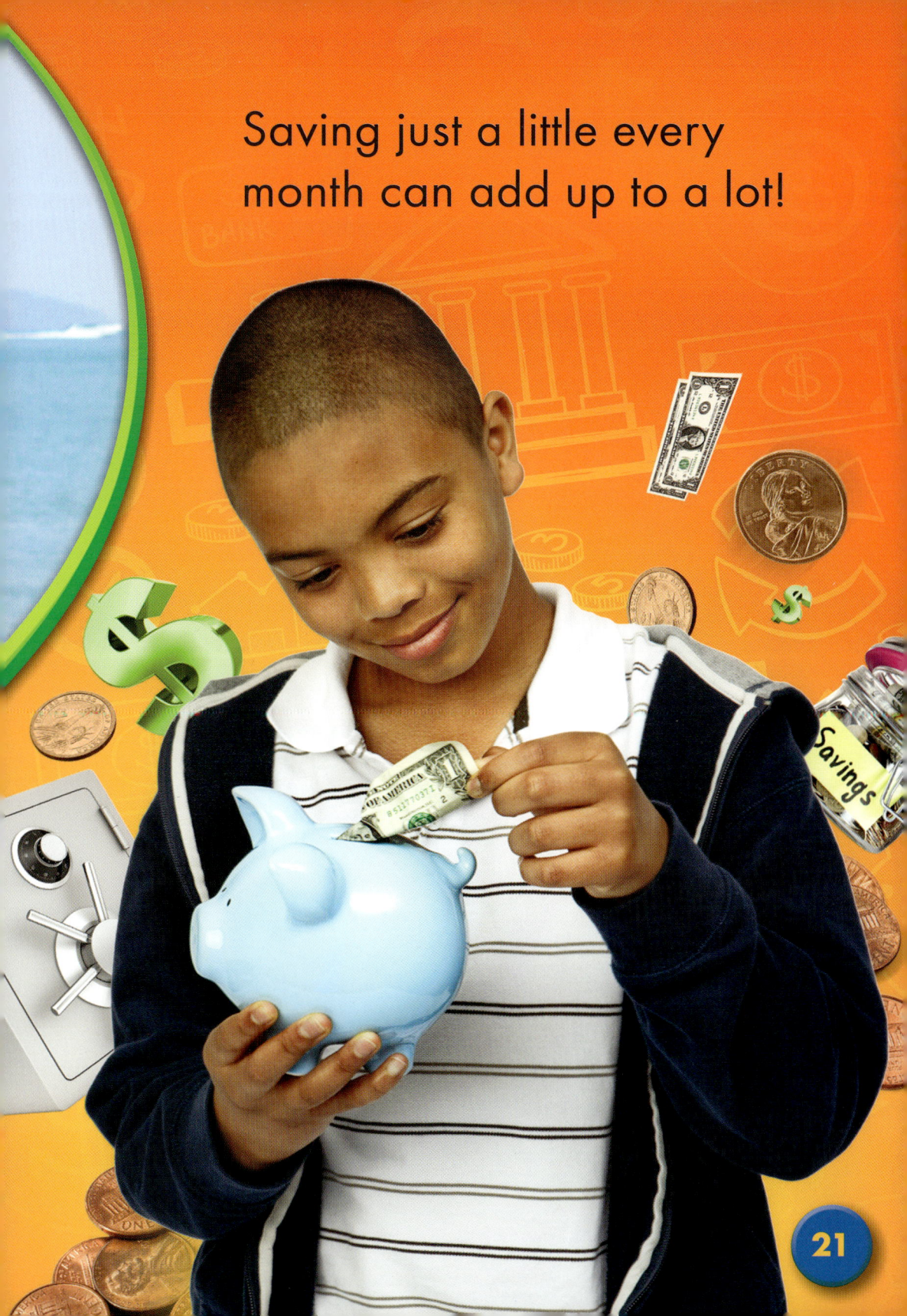

Saving just a little every month can add up to a lot!

Glossary

bank—a business where people keep their money

emergency fund—money that is saved to pay for unplanned costs

goal—something that a person aims for or works toward

interest—money that is paid to people for keeping their money in a bank account, savings bond, or other account

need—must have to live

sales—times when items are sold cheaper than usual

savings account—a bank account that pays people interest for keeping their money in it

savings bonds—money that is loaned to the government and then earns interest

want—would like to have

To Learn More

AT THE LIBRARY
Benjamin, Tina. *My Piggy Bank.* New York, N.Y.: Gareth Stevens Publishing, 2015.

Reina, Mary. *Save Money.* North Mankato, Minn.: Capstone Press, 2015.

Schwartz, Heather E. *Save Wisely.* Mankato, Minn.: Amicus, 2016.

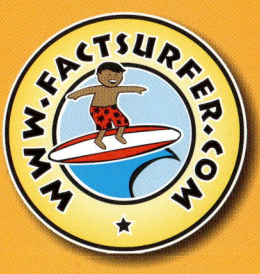

ON THE WEB
Learning more about saving money is as easy as 1, 2, 3.

1. Go to www.factsurfer.com.

2. Enter "saving money" into the search box.

3. Click the "Surf" button and you will see a list of related web sites.

With factsurfer.com, finding more information is just a click away.

Index

adults, 8
bank, 14
buy, 5, 6, 7, 16
car repairs, 9
college, 20
doctor visits, 9
earn, 11, 12, 17, 19
emergency fund, 8
future, 4
goal, 6
grow, 18, 19
house, 20
house projects, 9
interest, 19
kids, 10, 12
needs, 5
piggy bank, 11

sales, 7
savings account, 14, 15, 18
savings bonds, 16, 17, 18
spend, 7, 12
trips, 20
United States government, 16
unplanned costs, 5
wants, 5

The images in this book are reproduced through the courtesy of: Radius Images/ Corbis, cover, p. 21 (boy); Robyn Mackenzie, cover (top left bills), cover, p. 21 (pennies, dollar coins); Brostock, cover, p. 21 (safe); martan, cover, p. 21 (dollar signs); Africa Studio, cover, p. 21 (savings jar), p. 9 (paint); dibrova, cover (right bills); Brian A Jackson, cover, back cover (bottom piggybank); Dave and Les Jacobs/ Corbis, pp. 4-5; Monticello, p. 5 (food); Piotr Marcinski, p. 5 (clothes); Sean Locke Photography, p. 5 (school supplies); Tashka2000, p. 5 (games); LungLee, p. 5 (toys); Volodymyr Krasyuk, p. 5 (treats); GrayMark, p. 6 (left jar); Ryan DeBerardinis, p. 6 (right jar); JGI/ Jamie Grill/ Corbis, pp. 6-7, 18-19; Steven Frame, pp. 8-9; Tom Saga, p. 8 (label); vstock24, p. 9 (doctor visits); Rob Wilson, p. 9 (car repairs); victures, p. 9 (tools); Karen Roach, p. 10 (piggybank); Laura Doss/ Corbis, pp. 10-11; Michelle D. Milliman, p. 12; Tim Pannell/ Corbis, pp. 12-13; Hiya Images/ Corbis, p. 14; YinYang, p. 15; Comstock/ Exactostock/ Superstock, pp. 16-17; De-V, p. 19 (graph); Phil Date, pp. 20-21; nimon, p. 21 (one-dollar bills).